POSITION CHANGING FOR THE VIOLIN

NEIL MACKAY

Before beginning these exercises it is advisable to clean the neck of the violin with a damp cloth so that the surface of the wood is free from any dirt or perspiration which could prevent the hand from sliding smoothly up and down the instrument.

As the hand moves to 3rd Position, be careful to shift the thumb at the same time so that it occupies a similar position in relation to the fingers, as it did in 1st Position.

The change of position will produce a *glissando* at first as the finger slides over the string. This can be overcome by releasing the finger pressure slightly during the change of position, when, as the speed of the hand movement is increased, the *glissando* effect will gradually diminish.

1st FINGER MOVEMENT

A and D strings

T0088409

1 — 1 means keep the finger on the string.

1. HEBRIDEAN LULLABY

© Oxford University Press 1963

Printed in Great Britain
OXFORD UNIVERSITY PRESS, MUSIC DEPARTMENT, GREAT CLARENDON STREET, OXFORD OX2 6DP

Photocopying this copyright material is ILLEGAL.

E and A strings

2. THE FAIR ISLE

[4 bars introduction]

Allegretto

D and G strings

3. DEESIDE

[4 bars introduction]

Andantino

2nd FINGER MOVEMENT

A and D strings

4. MINUET

[4 bars introduction]

Grazioso

E and A strings

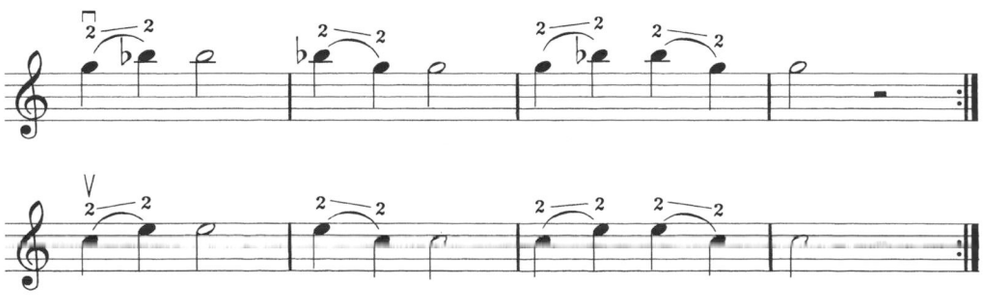

5. THE CLOWN'S DANCE

[2 bars introduction]

Allegro moderato

mp

p

mp

mf

cresc. poco a poco

pizz.

f

D and G strings

6. IN OLD MADRID

[2 bars introduction]

Andante

mp

mf

p

mp

3rd FINGER MOVEMENT

A string

7. A SPRING MORNING

[2 bars introduction]

Allegretto

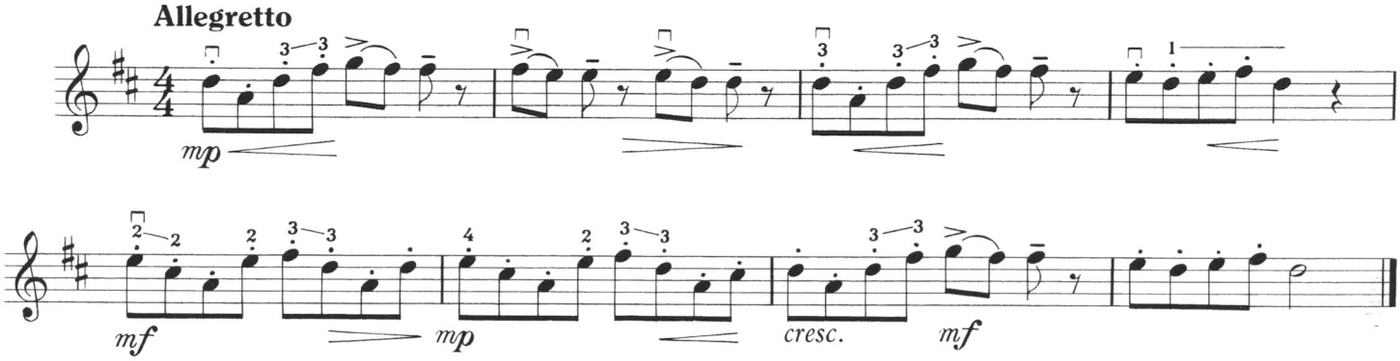

G string

8. EVENSONG

[4 bars introduction]

Lento

con sordini

E and D strings

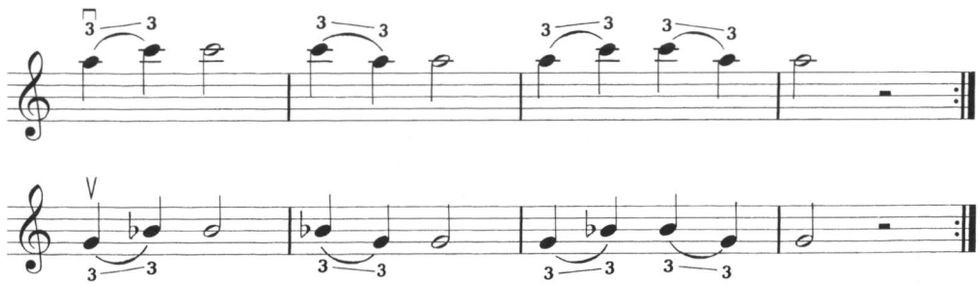

9. SNAKE ON A LADDER

[2 bars introduction]

Andantino

4th FINGER MOVEMENT

E and A strings

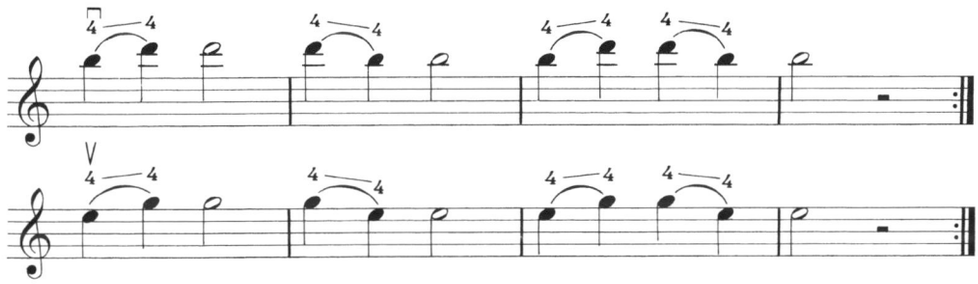

10. SPANISH SERENADE

[4 bars introduction]

Espressivo

D and G strings

11. IRISH LULLABY

CHANGING POSITION

From 1st Finger
to
2nd, 3rd, and 4th

The finger effecting the change of position should arrive at a guide note (𝅘𝅥𝅮) before the next note is played. With practice the *glissando* and guide note can be omitted.

Guide notes are not marked throughout the melodies, but should be used during each change of position.

D and G strings

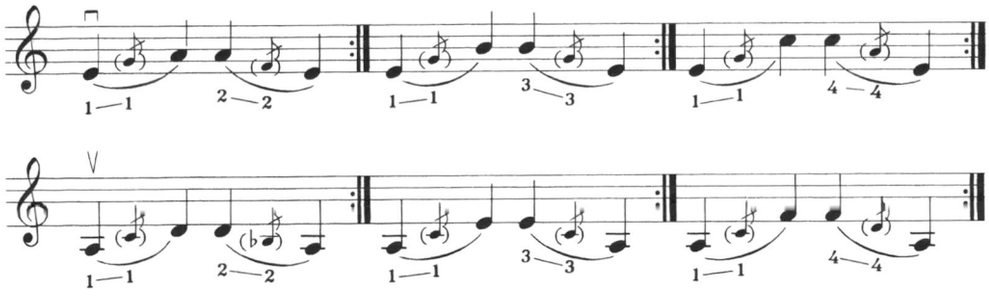

12. VALSE TRISTE

[4 bars introduction]

Moderato

p *cresc. poco a poco* *mf*

mp *p*

A and E strings

13. THE DANCING CLASS

[2 bars introduction]

Allegretto

mp *poco accel.*

mf (a tempo)

p *poco accel.* *a tempo*

mp *molto accel.* *f*

CHANGING POSITION
From 2nd and 3rd Fingers

E and A strings

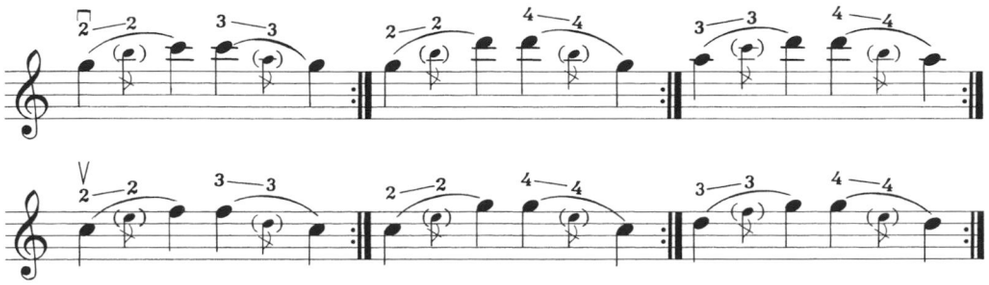

14. THE TROUBADOUR'S SONG

[2 bars introduction]

Andante con moto

p *mf* *f* *mf* *mp* *rall.* *pp* *a tempo* *poco rall.*

D and G strings

15. DANSE MACABRE

[1 bar introduction]

Misterioso

mp

p

poco a poco accel.

The last note of *Danse Macabre* is an Artificial Harmonic.

Stop E normally with the 1st finger, at the same time play A lightly with the pad of the 4th. This should produce a sound 2 octaves above the stopped note E.

HARMONICS

There are two types of harmonics playable on the violin. One is a NATURAL harmonic and the other ARTIFICIAL.

The following harmonics are natural, and are played half way up the string with the pad of the little finger.

Keep the left hand in 3rd Position and extend the fourth finger so that it rests lightly on the string. The violin will produce a flute-like note which is rather plaintive in sound.

16. REVEILLE

Play STACCATO notes OFF THE STRING in L.H. bow.

[4 bars introduction]

Vivo

mf *cresc.* *f*

17. ON PARADE

Play STACCATO in U.H. bow.

[1 bar introduction]

Allegro

mp *mf* *f*

18. TYROLEAN AIR

[3½ bars introduction]

Allegretto grazioso

mp *cresc.* *mf* *cresc.* *f* *dim.* *mp* *dim.* *poco rall.* *pp*

19. REVERIE

[1 bar introduction]

Teneramente

p

poco accel. *poco rall.* *mp a tempo*

mf *rall.*

MORE GUIDE NOTES

The following changes of position are frequently used by violinists. A good player never allows the left hand to leap from one position to another, unless it entails a move from an open string to a note in a higher position, or vice versa.

Remember always to use a GUIDE NOTE when effecting a position change, and avoid any intermediate sound between changes of position.

A and E strings

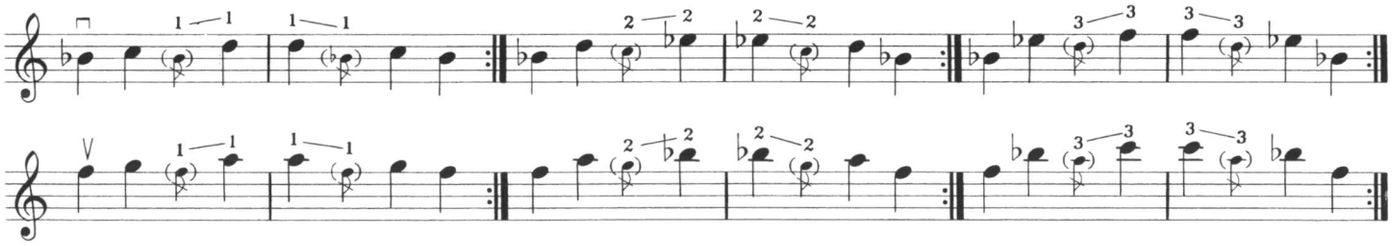

Practise also using a bow to each bar.

20. BUTTERFLIES

[2 bars introduction]

Allegro ritmico

p *mp* *cresc.* *f* *dim.* *mp* *p*